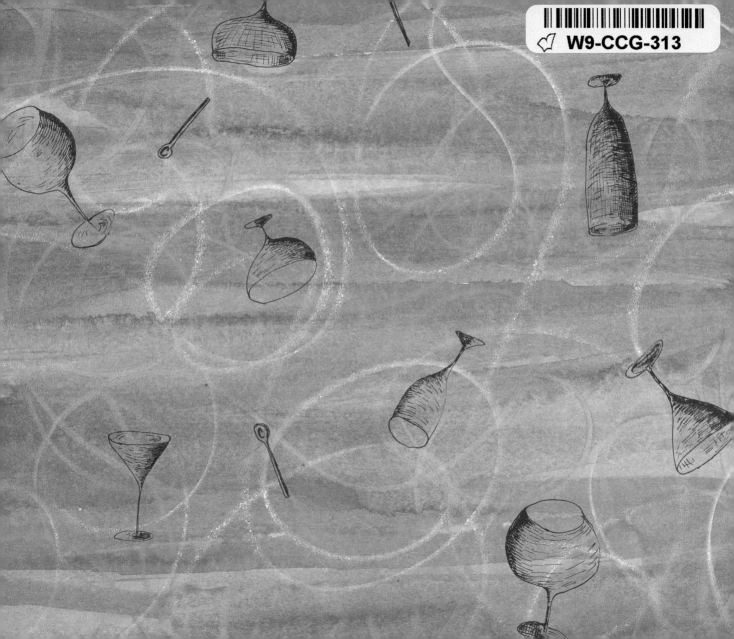

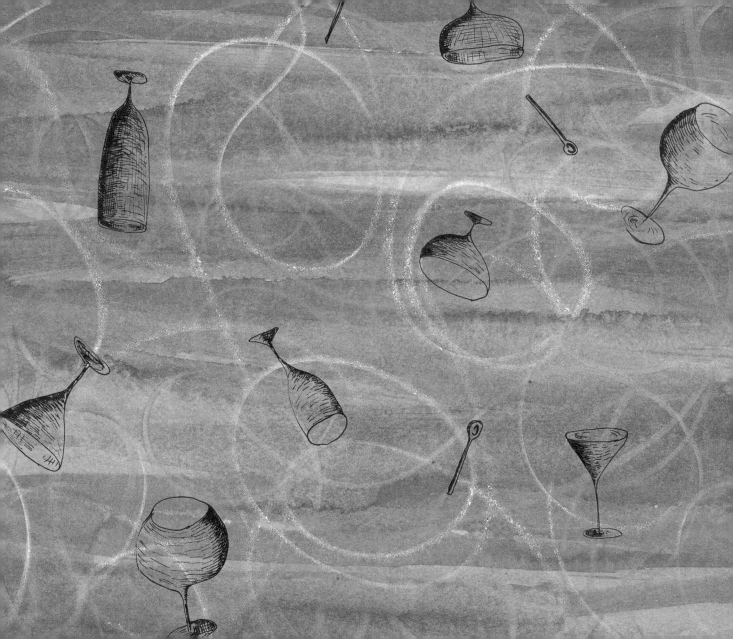

Granita Magic

GranitaMagic

Nadia Roden

ARTISAN
NEW YORK

Published by Artisan

A Division of Workman

Publishing

Company,

Inc.

708

Broadway,

New

York,

NY

10003-9555

www.artisanbooks.com

Book design by Vivian Ghazarian · Printed in Singapore · 10 9 8 7 6 5 4 3 2 1 · Library of Congress Cataloging-in-Publication Data on file

for

TERENCE DE PIETRO

c o n t

fruits

vegetables

contens

this book

started with a ginger granita. I made it while I was experimenting with desserts. It was so good and so intense that I kept making more and experimenting with other flavors. I tried classics from around the world and also created new combinations ranging from vegetables to flowers to wines. I started seeing everything as a potential granita!

Strangely, there were no cookbooks specifically about granitas, yet they are so delicious and fun to make. Here you'll find simple methods for making basic granitas, which can be made easily at home, without special equipment. I encourage you to improvise and experiment with flavors. After you've made a few, there is no limit to the possibilities!

I come from a family where the kitchen was the most exciting room in the house, so I often took my paints to work there. Now I find that the pleasures of cooking and tasting inspire me to paint. In this book

I have combined the two, making patterns and designs out of the ingredients for you to enjoy on the kitchen table while you are making your granita.

In creating this book, I have been particularly inspired by the textile designers of the 1950s, especially Lucienne Day, who playfully brought the organic forms of nature into the home via textile and wallpaper design.

when I told

people I was creating this book, they usually asked, "What is a granita?" Well, a granita looks and feels like icy snow, it is beautifully colored like glittering sequins, and it can be eaten at any time of day. Granita is a type of water ice that is looser and grainier in texture than its cousin, the sorbet, and it doesn't contain egg whites.

One of the advantages of granitas is that they are incredibly easy to make and require no special equipment. All you need is a fork, a tray, a freezer, and sometimes a food processor, a sieve, and a saucepan.

mystery

surrounds the origin of granita, which predates that of sorbet and ice cream by well over a thousand years. It is known, however, that syrups were combined with snow for the gustatory pleasure of Chinese emperors three thousand years ago. During the mid-first century A.D., the Roman emperor Nero regularly sent his servants up the Apennine Mountains to collect fresh glacier snow to mix with fruit pulps, flower petals, honeys, and wines for his banquets. The exact ingredients and proportions were kept secret—the "little grains" were to be enjoyed only in royal circles. Arab traders, who may have learned the method from the Chinese, famously took it to Sicily when they colonized the island in the ninth century. The idea spread throughout Italy and then to the rest of Europe and eventually to the Americas. Granita must be the original, classic "ice."

serving Granitas

It is traditional to serve a granita in a glass so you can enjoy its glittering color. Choose any glass shape that you love: a martini glass, a tall, plump, crystal goblet, a Champagne flute, even a tumbler. You can chill the glasses in the fridge before serving. I like to spoon the granitas into tall glasses with narrow stems that open up wide at the top.

You can top or accompany them with fresh or macerated fruits, herbs and flowers, a dollop of whipped cream, or a drizzle of a special spirit or liqueur.

Cookies are a perfect accompaniment to a granita. Traditional ones are langues de chat *(cats' tongues),* palmiers *(elephant ears),* tuiles *(almond cookies), and* boudoirs *(ladyfingers), as well as Breton butter cookies, madeleines, macaroons, and biscotti.*

There are no rules for what flavors to serve or when, but here are some suggestions to inspire you.

FOR DESSERT A sweet sensation of lightness at the end of a meal

FOR BREAKFAST Italians love to open a warm brioche and spoon in a coffee or fruit granita.

APPETIZER Cucumber & mint on a hot day

FOR BRUNCH Beet granita with vodka and sour cream

A PALATE CLEANSER The French serve citrus and vegetable granitas between courses to open the appetite and freshen the palate.

A WAY TO ENJOY SEASONAL FRUITS WHEN THEY ARE CHEAP AND PLENTIFUL Passion fruit with elephant ears

It is elegant to serve a granita at any time of day....

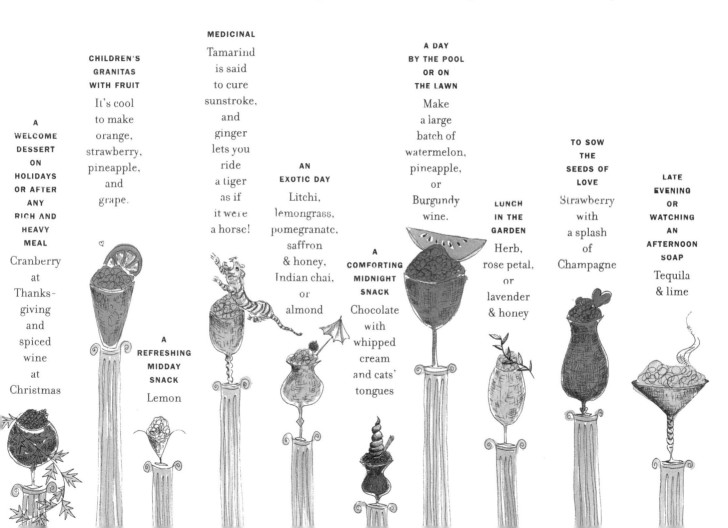

A WELCOME DESSERT ON HOLIDAYS OR AFTER ANY RICH AND HEAVY MEAL

Cranberry at Thanksgiving and spiced wine at Christmas

CHILDREN'S GRANITAS WITH FRUIT

It's cool to make orange, strawberry, pineapple, and grape.

A REFRESHING MIDDAY SNACK

Lemon

MEDICINAL

Tamarind is said to cure sunstroke, and ginger lets you ride a tiger as if it were a horse!

AN EXOTIC DAY

Litchi, lemongrass, pomegranate, saffron & honey, Indian chai, or almond

A COMFORTING MIDNIGHT SNACK

Chocolate with whipped cream and cats' tongues

A DAY BY THE POOL OR ON THE LAWN

Make a large batch of watermelon, pineapple, or Burgundy wine.

LUNCH IN THE GARDEN

Herb, rose petal, or lavender & honey

TO SOW THE SEEDS OF LOVE

Strawberry with a splash of Champagne

LATE EVENING OR WATCHING AN AFTERNOON SOAP

Tequila & lime

1.

Pour the granita mixture into a wide and shallow container.

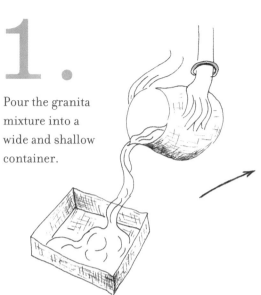

2.

Cover with a lid, foil, or plastic wrap. Freeze the mixture for an hour or two until it has frozen around the edge.

the Granita

(quick method)

This granita will have a different texture, a very fine grain, like slushy snow rather than icy morning snow.

1. Pour the granita mixture into ice trays, cover with plastic wrap, and allow to freeze solid.

2. Process the cubes in a food processor when you are ready to serve.

5.

It is best to eat the granita at once, but if you leave it in the freezer overnight or longer, just let it sit for about 10 minutes until it softens a little and then scrape it again with a fork to lighten the texture.

3.

Take the container out of the freezer and scrape the ice with a fork, mixing it from the edge into the center.

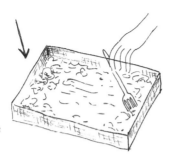

(classic)
method

4.

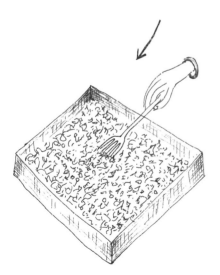

Repeat this scraping and mixing process every ½ hour or so (at least three times) until the entire mixture has turned into small, sequined ice flakes.

tips

· Chill the mixture in the fridge before freezing it.

· Freezers vary in temperature; make sure yours is at the coldest setting.

· The shallower your container, the quicker your granita will freeze. Try to keep the mixture less than $\frac{3}{4}$-inch deep.

· Use a nonreactive dish. Stainless steel conducts cold faster than plastic.

· Please adjust the sugar content to your own taste, remembering that the mixture will taste less sweet after freezing.

· Use regular granulated white sugar unless the ingredients specify superfine sugar.

· Chilling the container first will help speed the freezing.

· Granitas that are especially high in fruit pulp, sugar, or alcohol don't freeze solid. You can leave these mixtures in the freezer for hours, then scrape and mix them with a fork just before serving.

· Granitas that are high in alcohol have a melting texture and should be served straight from the freezer.

Fruits

Orange

serves 4 to 6

1¼ cups water

½ to ¾ cup sugar

Zest of 2 oranges

Juice of 6 large oranges

Juice of 1 lemon

3 to 4 teaspoons orange blossom water (optional)

Put the water, sugar, and orange zest in a saucepan and gently simmer until the sugar dissolves. Remove the saucepan from the heat to cool. Mix in the orange and lemon juices and the orange blossom water, if using.

To freeze the granita, follow the method on page 16.

YOU CAN SERVE THIS GRANITA WITH FRESH ORANGE SLICES. THE ORANGE BLOSSOM WATER ADDS A DELICATE MIDDLE EASTERN TOUCH. ALTERNATIVELY, YOU MAY PREFER TO ADD A FEW TABLESPOONS OF GRAND MARNIER OR TEQUILA.

EXPERIMENT WITH DIFFERENT VARIETIES OF ORANGES WHEN THEY ARE IN SEASON— SEVILLE OR BLOOD ORANGES, FOR EXAMPLE. ONE OF MY FAVORITES— MINNEOLA—IS ACTUALLY A TANGELO.

Pear

serves 4 to 6

YOU'LL FIND THAT
THIS IS AN ESPECIALLY
ELEGANT GRANITA.
AT THE TABLE, PASS
AROUND POIRE WILLIAM
OR ANOTHER PEAR
LIQUEUR FOR THOSE
WHO WANT TO
SPLASH SOME ON.

1¼ cups water

⅔ cup sugar

Juice of 1 lemon

5 large flavorful pears,
such as Bosc, D'Anjou, Bartlett, or Comice

Combine the water, sugar, and lemon juice in
a saucepan. Simmer until the sugar dissolves.

Meanwhile, peel, core, and cut the pears into
eighths. Slip them into the syrup to simmer,
covered, for 10 minutes or until they are tender.

Allow the mixture to cool slightly, then puree it
in a food processor. Taste and add more sugar
or lemon juice if needed.

To freeze the granita, follow the method on page 16.

Red Currant

serves 4 to 6

14 ounces red currants (about 3 cups)

2 cups water

$1/2$ cup plus 1 to 2 tablespoons sugar to taste

A squeeze of fresh lemon juice

Using the tines of a fork, strip the red currants from their stalks. Rinse the currants quickly in cold water and place them in a saucepan with the water and sugar. Simmer until the berries have burst. Set the pan aside and allow the mixture to cool.

Puree the mixture in a food processor, then strain it through a fine sieve to remove the seeds. Discard the seeds. Stir in the lemon juice to taste.

To freeze the granita, follow the method on page 16.

LOOK OUT FOR RED CURRANTS IN LATE JULY AND AUGUST WHEN THEY ARE IN SEASON. THEY MAKE A TANGY, SWEET, AND ZIPPY GRANITA.

Apple

serves 4 to 6

USE YOUR OWN JUICER OR TRY TO FIND THE BEST-QUALITY REAL PRESSED APPLE JUICE. THE GRATED APPLE ADDS A SPECIAL TEXTURE TO THIS GRANITA.

AT THE TABLE, YOU MIGHT PASS AROUND CALVADOS TO DRIZZLE OVER THE GRANITA AND SERVE A PLATE OF YOUR FAVORITE CHEESES TO ACCOMPANY IT.

1 to 2 tablespoons superfine sugar

3 cups fresh pressed pure apple juice

A squeeze of fresh lemon juice

1 apple, cored and peeled (my favorites are Russet, Golden Delicious, Cox, and Rome Beauty)

Pinch of ground cinnamon or nutmeg (optional)

Stir the sugar into the apple juice until the sugar dissolves. Add the lemon juice to taste and grate the apple into the mixture. If you like a little spice, add the cinnamon or nutmeg.

To freeze the granita, follow the method on page 16.

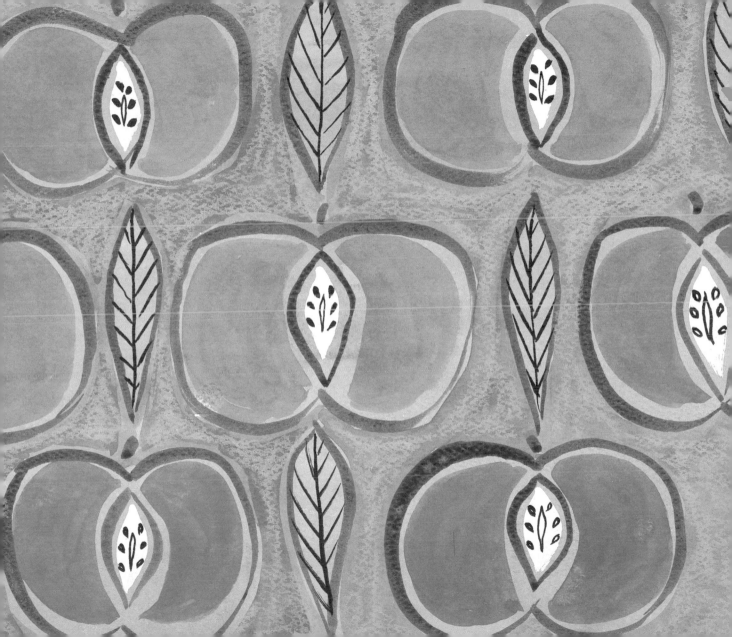

Festive
Cranberry

serves 4 to 6

IT'S CHRISTMAS EVERY DAY WITH THIS FESTIVE RUBY-RED SPECIAL. THIS GRANITA IS ALSO AN IDEAL CONCLUSION TO A HEAVY THANKSGIVING MEAL. YOU CAN SERVE IT WITH CRÈME FRAÎCHE OR WHIPPED CREAM WITH A LITTLE SUGAR AND COINTREAU WHIPPED IN.

$3^{1}/_{4}$ cups water

1 generous cup sugar

$2^{1}/_{2}$ cups fresh (or frozen) cranberries

Zest of 1 orange

Juice of 2 oranges

3 tablespoons lemon juice

Simmer the water and sugar together in a medium saucepan. When the sugar has dissolved, drop in the cranberries and simmer for another 3 to 5 minutes or until the berries have burst.

Allow the mixture to cool, then puree to a liquid in a food processor.

Pour the mixture through a fine sieve, stirring with a spoon. Discard the solids. Stir in the orange zest, orange juice, and lemon juice.

To freeze the granita, follow the method on page 16.

Classic
Lemon

serves 4 to 6

3 cups water

1 heaping cup sugar

Zest of 2 lemons

Juice of 6 large lemons

Boil the water in a saucepan with the sugar and lemon zest. When the sugar dissolves, remove from the heat.

Mix in the lemon juice and allow the mixture to cool.

To freeze the granita, follow the method on page 16.

PLEASE MAKE THIS. IT'S A FAVORITE CLASSIC FROM SICILY. IT IS ALSO THE GRANITA MOST COMMONLY SERVED BETWEEN COURSES TO RENEW THE APPETITE. GARNISHED WITH MINT LEAVES, IT IS ONE OF THE MOST INTENSE AND REFRESHING GRANITAS.

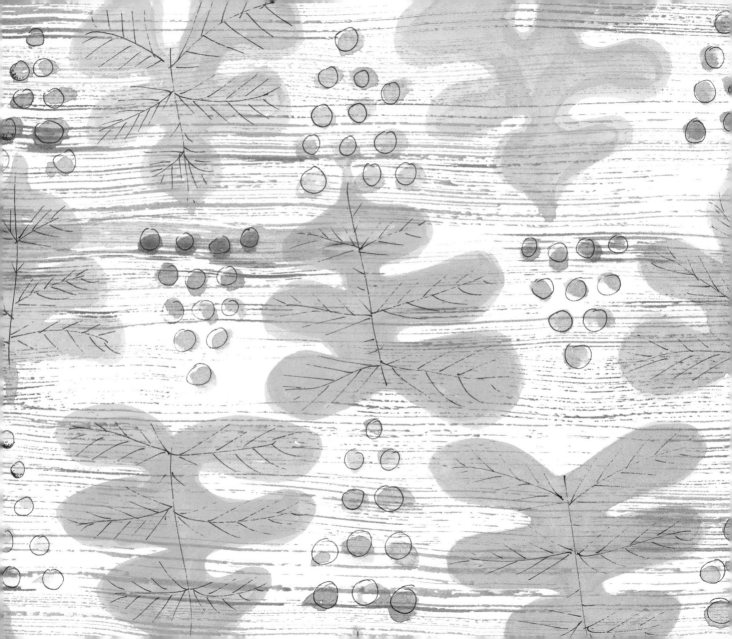

Green Grape

serves 4 to 6

2 pounds green grapes

2 to 4 tablespoons superfine sugar

3 to 4 tablespoons fresh lemon juice

1 cup white wine
(Muscadet wine if you are using muscat grapes)
or water

Rinse the grapes, place them in a food processor, and whiz until smooth, at least 1 minute. Set the mixture aside for at least 20 minutes so the skins can flavor the juice.

Strain through a fine sieve, pressing the solids down with a spoon; discard the skins. Mix in the sugar, lemon juice, and wine. Taste and adjust sweetness, adding a little more sugar if needed.

To freeze the granita, follow the method on page 16.

THE RICH FLAVOR OF FRESHLY PRESSED GRAPES IS NOTHING LIKE THE GRAPE JUICE YOU FIND IN A SHOP. FOR A GRANITA WITH A HEAVENLY FLORAL BOUQUET, USE MUSCAT GRAPES. SAVE A FEW GRAPES TO SLICE OVER THE GRANITA FOR A BEAUTIFUL PRESENTATION.

Strawberry

serves 4 to 6

1 cup water

3/4 cup sugar or to taste

1 1/2 pounds sweet ripe strawberries
(about 5 heaping cupfuls)

1 cup fresh orange juice

Juice of 1 1/2 lemons

Simmer the water with the sugar for a minute in a medium saucepan. Remove from the heat and allow to cool.

Briefly rinse the strawberries and hull them. Blend the berries to a puree in a food processor.

Mix in the sugar syrup and the orange and lemon juices. Taste and add more sugar if needed.

To freeze the granita, follow the method on page 16.

BE SURE TO
MAKE THIS WHEN
STRAWBERRIES
ARE SWEET AND
PLENTIFUL.

FOR ADDED ROMANCE
REDUCE THE WATER
TO 1/4 CUP AND
STIR IN 1 1/2 CUPS
CHAMPAGNE
(IT CAN BE FLAT)
BEFORE FREEZING.
FOR A MORE INTENSE
STRAWBERRY
FLAVOR, OMIT THE
ORANGE JUICE.

I LIKE TO TOP THIS
WITH A FEW FRESH
STRAWBERRIES AND
MINT LEAVES.

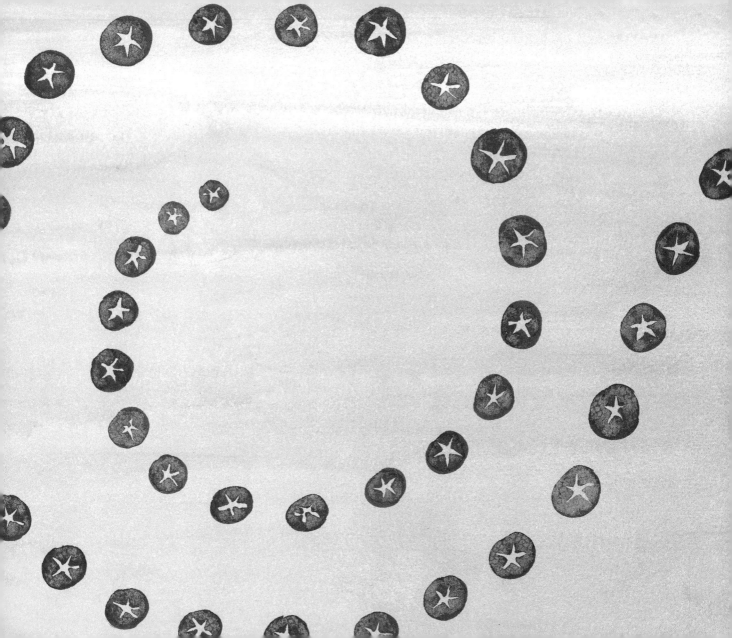

Blueberry

serves 4 to 6

¾ cup sugar

2 tablespoons peeled and
very finely chopped fresh ginger (optional)

1 pound blueberries (about 3 heaping cups)

5 tablespoons lime juice

1 cup water

Put the sugar in a food processor. Add the ginger, and puree to a paste. Add the blueberries, lime juice, and water and puree to a liquid.

Strain through a fine sieve, stirring and pressing with a spoon. Discard the solids.

To freeze the granita, follow the method on page 16.

BLUEBERRY GRANITA HAS A WONDERFULLY SUBTLE FLAVOR. ADDING GINGER WILL GIVE IT A LITTLE ZING WITHOUT MASKING ITS DELICACY.

Litchi
& Lime

serves 4 to 6

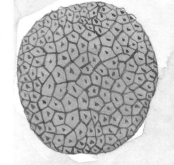

CANNED, PITTED LITCHIS IN SYRUP ARE EXCELLENT FOR THIS GRANITA. THE ADDITION OF GINGER OR LIME LEAVES (AVAILABLE AT SPECIALTY FOOD STORES) ONLY ENHANCES THE DELICATE PERFUME. YOU CAN ALSO ENJOY THIS TREAT WITHOUT THE EXTRA FLAVORING. TOP IT WITH CHOPPED PRESERVED GINGER IF YOU LIKE.

6 fresh lime leaves or 2 tablespoons peeled freshly grated ginger (optional)

1 cup water

One 20-ounce can litchis in syrup

Juice of 1 lime

2 to 6 tablespoons superfine sugar, depending on the sweetness of the litchi syrup

If using lime leaves or ginger, place them in a saucepan with water. Drain the syrup from the litchi can, reserving the litchis. Add the syrup to the saucepan and heat to just boiling. Remove the pan from the heat and set it aside to cool to room temperature.

Remove the leaves and place the mixture along with and the litchis in a food processor. Puree until smooth. Strain through a fine sieve, pressing hard to extract all the juice. Stir in the lime juice and sugar to taste.

To freeze the granita, follow the method on page 16.

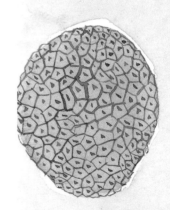

FRUITS

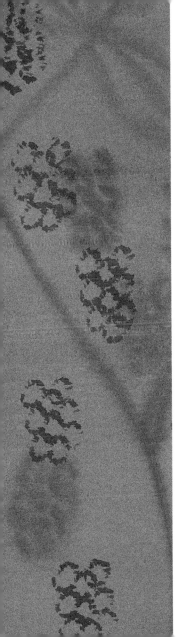

Very
Raspberry

serves 4 to 6

1¹/₂ cups water

¹/₂ cup sugar

³/₄ pound fresh (or frozen) raspberries
(about 2 generous cups)

¹/₂ cup raspberry preserves (optional)

2¹/₂ tablespoons fresh lemon juice

Bring the water and sugar to a boil in a saucepan. Reduce the heat to a simmer and, when the sugar has dissolved, stir the raspberries into the syrup and allow to cool.

Place the preserves, if using, in a food processor along with the raspberry syrup and puree.

Press the mixture through a fine sieve, discarding the seeds. Stir in the lemon juice.

To freeze the granita, follow the method on page 16.

THE RASPBERRY PRESERVES GIVE THIS GRANITA A LUXURIOUS RICHNESS.

IF YOU LIKE, DRIZZLE A LITTLE CRÈME DE CASSIS OVER THE GRANITA AND SERVE IT WITH TUILES AND A DOLLOP OF CRÈME FRAÎCHE.

Fragrant Melon

serves 4 to 6

YOU CAN USE ANY RIPE
FLAVORFUL MELON,
SUCH AS CANTALOUPE,
HONEYDEW, OR MUSK, FOR
THIS GRANITA. MY OWN
FAVORITE IS THE HIGHLY
PERFUMED CHANTERAIS
CANTALOUPE.

PORT IS A WONDERFUL
MATCH WITH MELON.
YOU MAY PREFER TO WAIT
AND DRIZZLE THE PORT
OVER THE GRANITA AT
THE TABLE.

1 very ripe, sweet fragrant melon

$1/4$ cup superfine sugar

Juice of 1 lemon

6 to 8 tablespoons port (optional)

Halve the melon and scoop out the seeds.
Cut the flesh away from the rind and slice the
flesh into a food processor.

Place the rest of the ingredients in the food
processor and blend until smooth. Taste and
add more sugar if needed

To freeze the granita, follow the method on page 16.

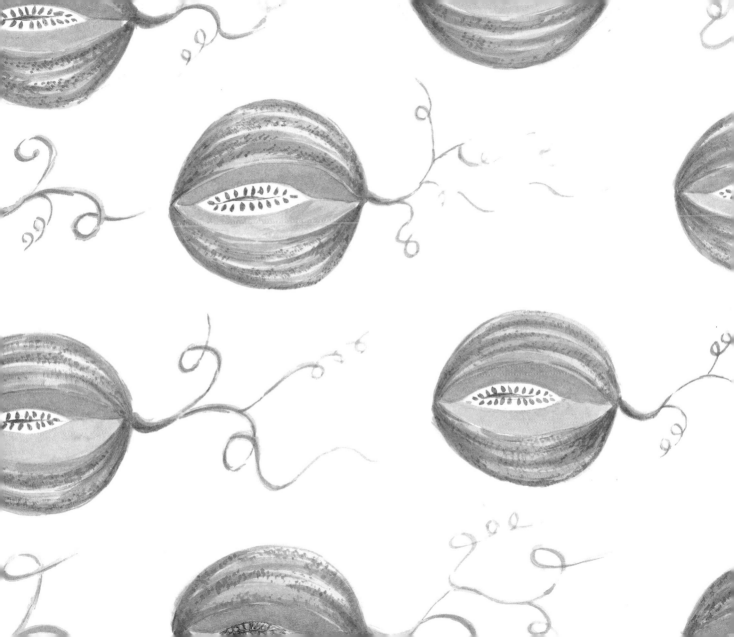

Apricot

serves 4 to 6

1 1/4 cups water

1/2 cup sugar

Juice of 1/2 lemon

1 pound ripe apricots

Simmer the water, sugar, and lemon juice in a medium saucepan until the sugar dissolves.

Meanwhile, rinse the apricots, cut them in half, and remove the stones. Simmer the apricots in the syrup for 5 to 10 minutes or until tender.

Allow the mixture to cool, then puree in a food processor.

To freeze the granita, follow the method on page 16.

I LOVE THE RICH COLOR AND TANGY FLAVOR OF THIS GRANITA.

TRY IT WITH A GLASS OF SAUTERNES, MUSCAT, OR ANOTHER SWEET WHITE WINE.

Tropical
Pineapple

serves 4 to 6

TRY THIS SUNNY,
LUMINOUS TREAT WITH
A SPLASH OF RUM.

1 large pineapple

Juice and zest of 1 lemon or lime

4 to 8 tablespoons sugar,
depending on the sweetness of the pineapple

One 13-ounce can coconut milk
or 1½ cups fresh orange juice or water

Cut the crown off and halve the pineapple lengthwise. Cut away the peel with a large, sharp knife and pare out any remaining eyes. Slice each half into 2 pieces lengthwise, cut away and discard the hard core, and cube the flesh.

Place the pineapple pieces in a food processor with the lemon juice and zest, sugar, and coconut milk, and process to a fine puree.

Strain the puree through a fine sieve, pressing down with a spoon. Discard the solids. Taste and add more sugar if needed.

To freeze the granita, follow the method on page 16.

Gooseberry

serves 4 to 6

1 pound gooseberries (about 3 heaping cups)

3 cups water

²/₃ to 1 cup sugar to taste,
depending on the tartness of the gooseberries

Juice of ¹/₂ lemon

3 tablespoons elderflower cordial or muscat
(optional)

Wash the gooseberries (there's no need to remove the stems and tails). Pour the water and sugar into a medium saucepan and simmer to dissolve the sugar. Stir the berries into the syrup and simmer until they are tender.

Puree the mixture in a food processor. Press the puree through a fine sieve, discarding the skins and seeds. Mix in the lemon juice and the elderflower cordial, if using.

To freeze the granita, follow the method on page 16.

COMBINING GOOSEBERRIES
WITH ELDERFLOWER
IS CLASSICALLY ENGLISH.

THE VERY SHARP, GREEN
GOOSEBERRIES USED
FOR COOKING ARE THE
TASTIEST BUT NEED QUITE
A BIT MORE SUGAR THAN
THE SWEETER, MORE
GOLDEN ONES.

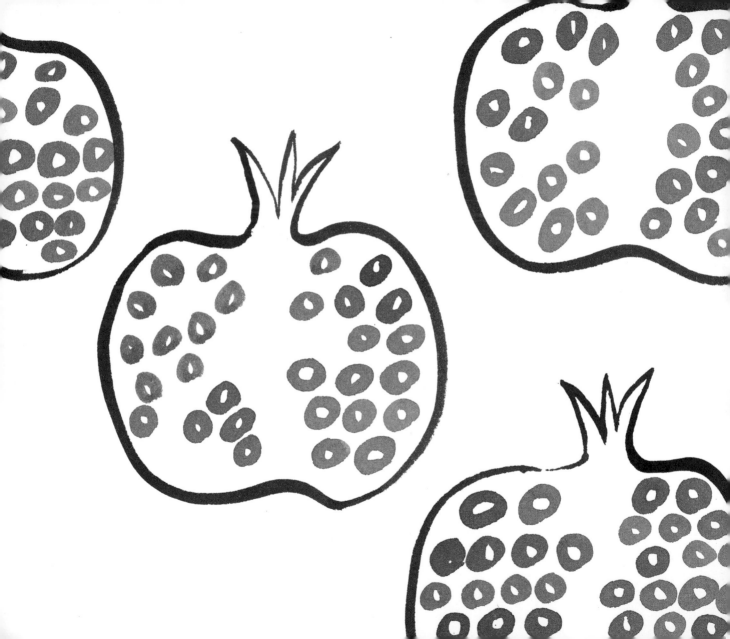

Pomegranate

serves 4 to 6

4 to 6 tablespoons sugar

$1/2$ cup water

4 large ripe pomegranates (see sidebar)

$1^1/2$ tablespoons rose water (optional)

A squeeze of fresh lemon juice

Simmer the sugar and water in a saucepan. When the sugar is dissolved, remove the saucepan from the heat.

Cut the fruit in half, collecting the juice that spills out. Scoop the seeds and their liquid into a food processor, removing any bitter membrane. Process into a pulpy juice.

Pour the juice into a fine sieve and squeeze the remaining pulp tight with your hands to extract all the liquid. Discard the solids.

Mix in the sugar syrup and rose water, if using, and add the lemon juice to your taste.

To freeze the granita, follow the method on page 16.

A BIBLICAL FRUIT WITH A VERY SPECIAL FLAVOR. IT IS WORTH EXTRACTING THE JUICE. TO HELP RELEASE THE JUICES, ROLL THE POMEGRANATES ON YOUR WORK SURFACE, PRESSING DOWN WITH THE PALMS OF YOUR HANDS.

CHOOSE HEAVY POMEGRANATES WITH FRESH-LOOKING PINK OR FUCHSIA SKINS THAT ARE NOT CRACKED OR DRIED OUT.

Passion Fruit

serves 4 to 6

THE PASSION FLOWER
PLANT IS SAID TO
REPRESENT THE FIVE
WOUNDS OF CHRIST.
I LOVE THE INTENSE,
HEAVENLY SCENT OF
ITS FRUIT.

YOU CAN ALSO MIX IN
1 CUP OF FRESH
ORANGE JUICE AS WELL,
AND THE FLAVOR OF
PASSION FRUIT WILL
STILL DOMINATE.
THIS IS LOVELY ON ITS
OWN OR SERVED WITH
WHIPPED CREAM.

2 cups water

1/2 cup sugar

6 to 8 ripe passion fruits

A squeeze of fresh lemon juice

Make a syrup by gently boiling the water with
the sugar in a medium saucepan. When the
sugar dissolves, take the pan off the heat to
cool a little.

Cut the passion fruits in half and scoop out
the pulp into a food processor. Give it a quick
whiz to separate the flesh from the hard seeds.
Strain the mixture, discarding the seeds,
and mix with the sugar syrup and lemon juice
to taste.

To freeze the granita, follow the method on page 16.

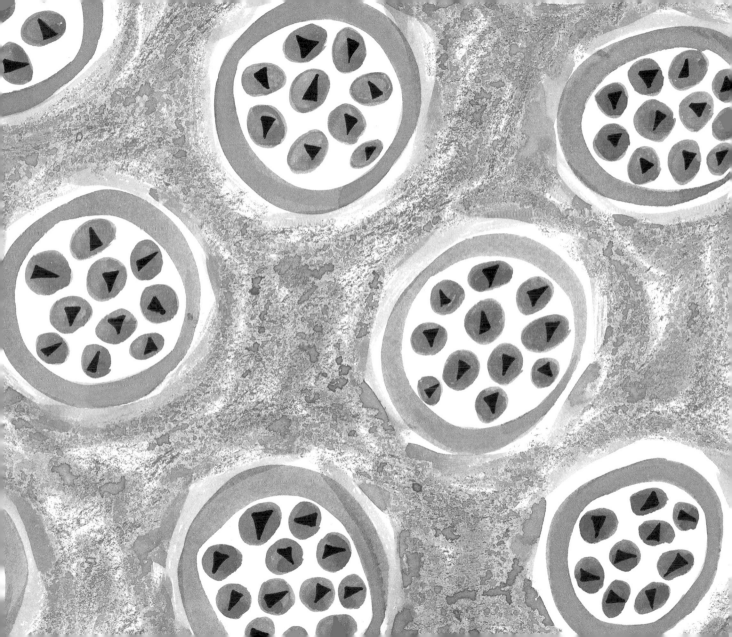

Pl^um

serves 4 to 6

1½ pounds plums

1 cup water

½ cup plus 1 to 2 tablespoons sugar

Juice of 1 lemon

Rinse the plums, halve them, and remove the stones. In a medium saucepan, combine the plums with the water, sugar, and lemon juice to taste. Simmer for 10 to 15 minutes or until the plums break apart.

Press the mixture through a fine sieve, discarding the solids left behind.

To freeze the granita, follow the method on page 16.

THIS GRANITA HAS A MELTING TEXTURE AND IS SLIGHTLY TART AND SWEET AT THE SAME TIME. WHEN I HAVE TIME, I LIKE TO CHOOSE THREE VARIETIES OF PLUMS AND POACH THEM SEPARATELY. THEIR COLORS ARE BEAUTIFUL SERVED SIDE BY SIDE.

SERVE, IF YOU LIKE, WITH PLUM BRANDY AND ALMOND TUILES.

Blackberry

serves 4 to 6

BOTH FRANCE AND
GERMANY PRODUCE FINE
CRÈMES DE MÛRE,
A BLACKBERRY LIQUEUR.
YOU CAN SUBSTITUTE
CRÈME DE CASSIS,
WHICH IS MADE FROM
RUM AND BLACK
CURRANTS.

IF YOU DECIDE NOT TO
MIX THE CRÈME DE MÛRE
INTO THE GRANITA,
YOU CAN ALWAYS DRIZZLE
IT OVER AT THE TABLE.

2 cups water

$1/2$ cup plus 1 tablespoon sugar

1 pound fresh (or frozen) blackberries
(about $3^1/2$ cups)

Juice of 2 lemons

4 tablespoons crème de mûre (optional)

Simmer the water and sugar in a medium
saucepan until the sugar dissolves. Rinse the
blackberries and quickly ease them into the
syrup. Simmer for about 3 minutes until
the berry juices are released. Remove from
the heat and allow to cool.

Puree the mixture in a food processor, then
strain through a fine sieve to remove the seeds.
Discard the seeds. Mix in the lemon juice and
crème de mûre, if using.

To freeze the granita, follow the method on page 16.

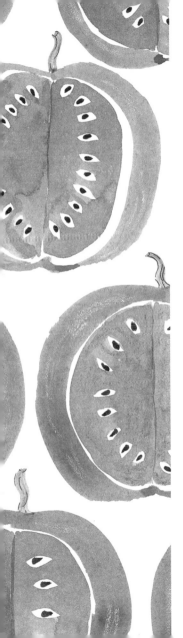

Watermelon

serves 4 to 6

½ cup water

5 to 7 tablespoons sugar

½ large watermelon (5 pounds of flesh)

Juice and zest of 2 limes

Put the water and sugar in a saucepan and bring to a low boil. When the sugar has dissolved, remove the pan from the heat.

Cut the rind off the watermelon, then cut the flesh into 2-inch chunks.

Puree the melon chunks in batches in a food processor. Press the puree through a sieve; discard the seeds and fibers. Stir the syrup and the lime juice and zest into the melon liquid.

To freeze the granita, follow the method on page 16.

EVERYBODY MAKE THIS! IT'S EVEN BETTER THAN BITING INTO A WEDGE OF FRESH WATERMELON. YOU CAN DRIZZLE COINTREAU OR TEQUILA OVER THIS GRANITA.

Sweet & Sour Cherry

serves 4 to 6

THE SEASON FOR SOUR
CHERRIES IS ONLY A
FEW WEEKS LONG, SO
THEY ARE VERY
DIFFICULT TO FIND
FRESH. HOWEVER, THE
ONES PRESERVED IN
SYRUP IN A JAR WILL
DO VERY WELL FOR
THIS QUICK AND
FLAVORFUL GRANITA.
IF YOU WISH, YOU CAN
DRIZZLE THE LIQUEUR
OVER THE GRANITA AND
SERVE THE GRANITA
WITH TUILLES.

1/2 cup water

4 to 6 tablespoons sugar

1 pound preserved pitted sour Morello cherries
in syrup

Juice of 1/2 to 1 lemon

3 to 4 tablespoons kirsch, maraschino,
or crème de cassis (optional)

In a medium saucepan, stir together the water
and sugar. Simmer over low heat until the sugar
dissolves, then remove from the heat. Set aside
to cool slightly.

Pour the cherries and their syrup into a food
processor, add the sugar syrup, and blend
to a light puree.

Press the mixture through a fine sieve. Mix in
the lemon juice and kirsch, if using. Taste and
add more sugar if needed.

To freeze the granita, follow the method on page 16.

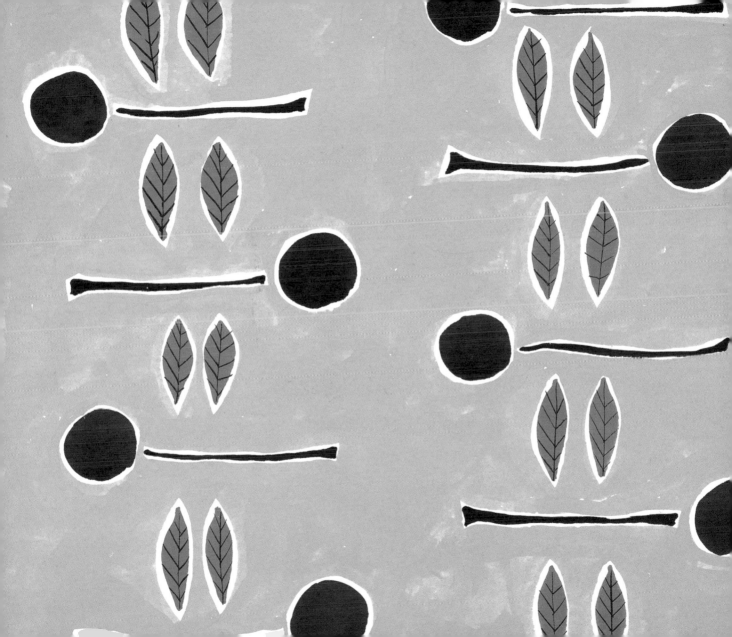

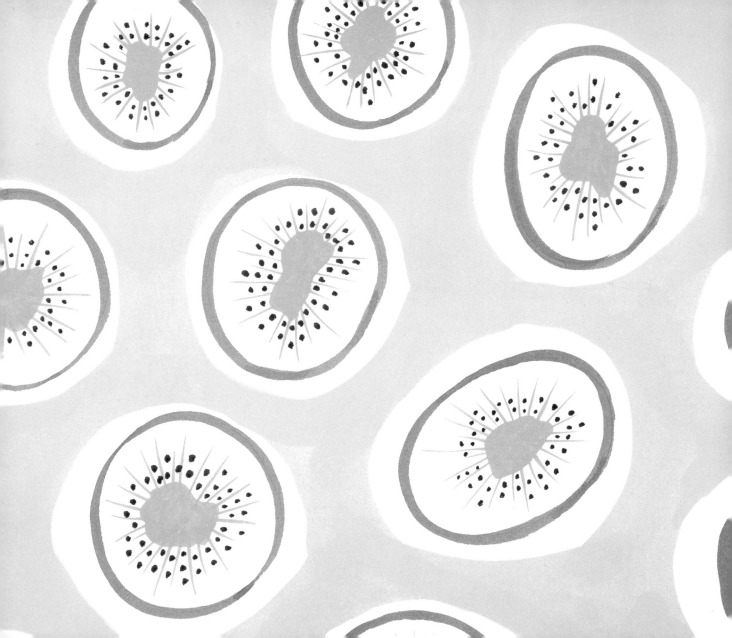

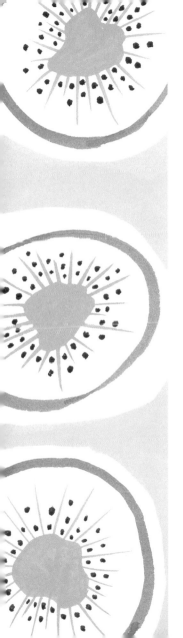

Kiwi

serves 4 to 6

½ cup water

½ cup sugar

6 to 8 soft and well-ripened kiwis

3 tablespoons fresh lemon juice

1½ tablespoons very finely grated
fresh ginger (optional)

Combine the water and sugar in a medium saucepan and heat until the sugar dissolves. Remove the pan from the heat and allow the sugar syrup to cool.

Cut the kiwis in half crosswise. Cradle each half in your palm while you scoop out the flesh with a spoon. Avoid the hard white core; discard the skins.

Place the kiwi directly into a food processor with the syrup, lemon juice, and ginger, if using. Blend to a rough puree.

To freeze the granita, follow the method on page 16.

THESE HAIRY BROWN GLOBES WITH TANGY EMERALD GREEN FLESH WERE ORIGINALLY CALLED YANG TAO OR CHINESE GOOSEBERRIES. THEY ARE FULL OF VITAMIN C AND POTASSIUM— SAID TO BE A TONIC FOR WOMEN AFTER CHILDBIRTH.

THE OPTIONAL GINGER ADDS A LIVELY ACCENT.

Ruby
Grapefruit
& Campari

serves 4 to 6

A PARTY FAVORITE!
YOU CAN SERVE
THIS GRANITA BEFORE
DINNER INSTEAD
OF AN APERITIF OR
AFTERWARD
AS A DESSERT.

1¼ cups water

Zest of 1 ruby grapefruit

½ to ¾ cup sugar

Juice of 4 ruby grapefruits (5 cups)

9 tablespoons Campari

Gently heat the water, zest, and sugar in a saucepan until the sugar has dissolved.

Take the pan off of the heat, mix in the grapefruit juice and the Campari, and set aside to cool.

To freeze the granita, follow the method on page 16.

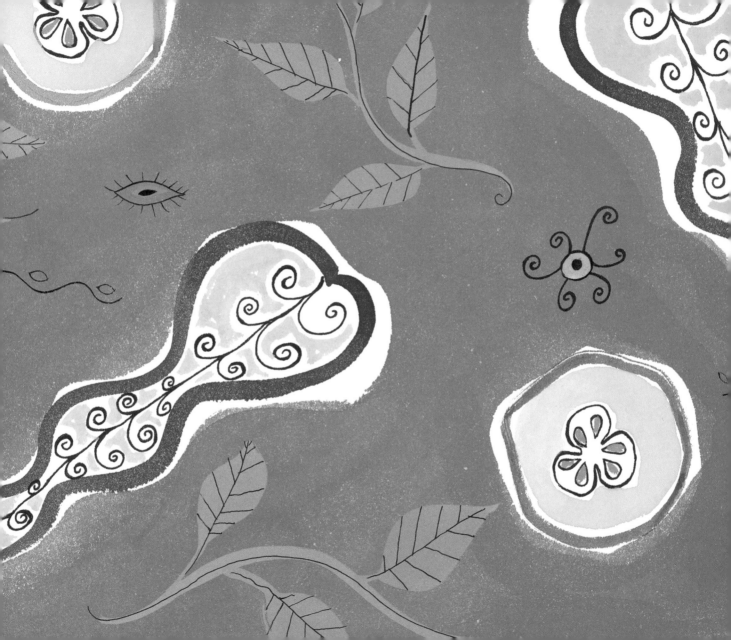

Vegetables

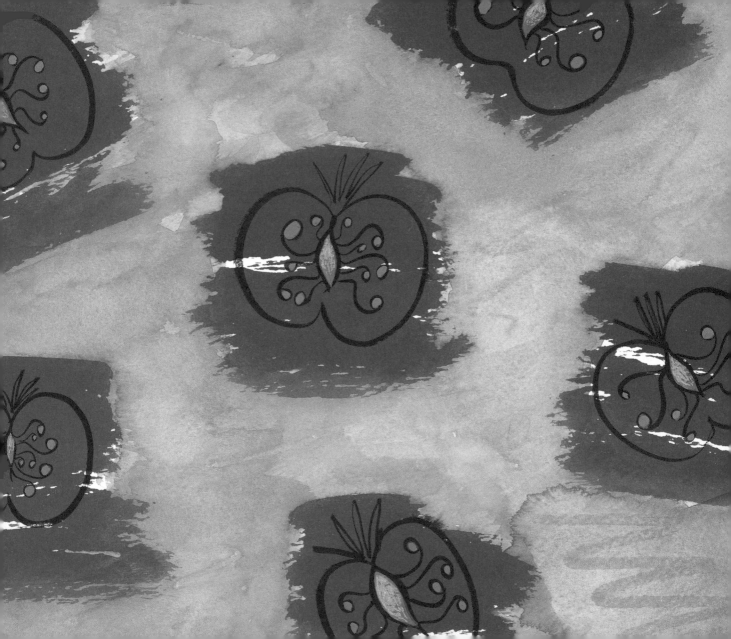

Tomato
& Basil

serves 4 to 6

---

2 pounds ripe sweet tomatoes, peeled
(see sidebar)

1 tablespoon sugar

1 clove garlic, finely chopped

2 to 3 teaspoons coarsely ground black pepper

2 tablespoons fresh lemon juice

Large handful of basil leaves, finely chopped

$1/2$ to $3/4$ teaspoon salt

Quarter the tomatoes and puree in a food processor with the sugar and garlic.

Strain through a sieve to discard the seeds, then stir in the pepper, lemon juice, basil, and salt to taste.

Let the mixture chill in the refrigerator for at least 20 minutes to allow the flavors to develop.

To freeze the granita, follow the method on page 16.

SERVE THIS ANDALUSIAN-INSPIRED GRANITA AS AN APERITIF OR A MID-MEAL PALATE CLEANSER. YOU CAN TOP IT WITH CHOPPED PEPPERS AND CUCUMBERS.

TO PEEL TOMATOES, PLUNGE THEM IN BOILING WATER FOR A MINUTE. THE SKINS WILL THEN SLIP OFF EASILY.

Carrot
& Orange

serves 4 to 6

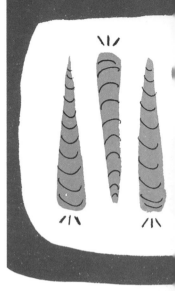

BUY FRESHLY SQUEEZED
JUICES FROM A
MARKET IF YOU DON'T
HAVE A JUICER.
FRESH PINEAPPLE JUICE
ALSO MAKES A SHARP-
TASTING COMBINATION
WITH CARROT JUICE.

I LIKE TO SQUEEZE ON
LEMON OR LIME JUICE
WHEN SERVING
TO GIVE IT A TWANG.

2 cups carrot juice

1¹⁄₂ cups fresh orange juice (2 large juice oranges)

2 tablespoons honey

Mix the carrot juice with the orange juice and stir in the honey until it dissolves. The honey will mix in more easily if the juices are near room temperature.

To freeze the granita, follow the method on page 16.

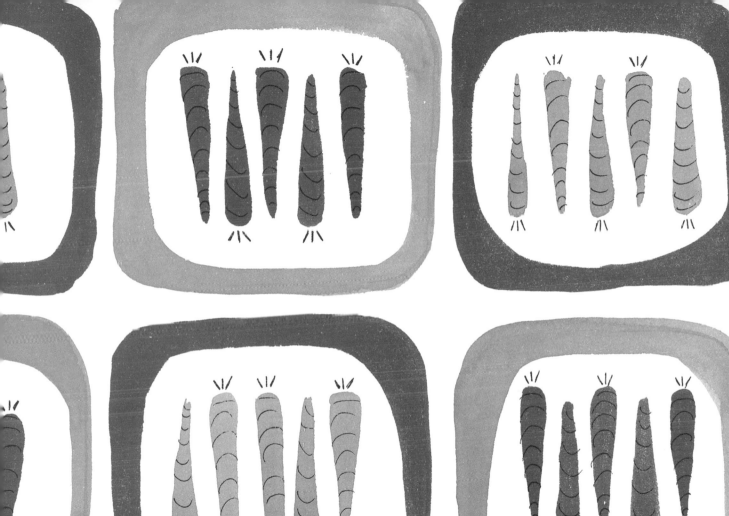

Balsamic
Red Pepper

serves 4 to 6

2 pounds roasted red bell peppers (5 large)
(see sidebar)

1¹/₂ cups water

1 tablespoon sugar

2 tablespoons balsamic vinegar

2 tablespoons fresh lemon juice

Salt and plenty of freshly ground black pepper

2 cloves garlic, crushed (optional)

A handful of chopped cilantro (optional)

Blend the roasted peppers, their juices,
and all the remaining ingredients in the food
processor. Taste and add more sugar, lemon
juice, or seasonings if needed.

To freeze the granita, follow the method on page 16.

SERVE THIS GARDEN
DELIGHT AS AN APPETIZER
OR MID-MEAL PALATE
CLEANSER. I LIKE TO SERVE
IT ON A BED OF ARUGULA.

TO ROAST BELL PEPPERS,
GRILL OR BAKE THEM
UNTIL BLACKENED. LEAVE
THEM TO COOL IN A
PLASTIC BAG (THE STEAM
WILL LOOSEN THEIR
SKINS). WHEN THEY ARE
COOL, PEEL OFF THEIR
SKINS, SAVING ALL THE
JUICES, AND SCRAPE OUT
THE SEEDS WITH A SHARP
KNIFE. (AVOID RINSING
THE PEPPERS, SINCE THIS
WASHES AWAY MUCH OF
THEIR FLAVOR.)

Horseradish

serves 4 to 6

SERVE THIS
EYE-OPENING GRANITA
WITH OYSTERS,
SCALLOPS, CRAB,
SHRIMP, AND OTHER
FAVORITE SEAFOOD.
IT'S ALSO GREAT
SERVED BETWEEN
COURSES.

THE MUSCATEL VINEGAR
OFFERS A RICH
AROMATIC FLAVOR.

1 cup peeled and chopped horseradish

7 tablespoons white muscat wine vinegar (muscatel)
or other white wine vinegar

$3^1/2$ cups water

A sprinkling of salt

1 to 2 tablespoons sugar

Put the chopped horseradish, vinegar, and 1 cup of the water in a food processor and blend to a puree. Add the remaining water, but turn your face away when you do so; the vapors will make your eyes water! Blend further to combine.

Allow the mixture to sit for 10 minutes, then strain it through a fine sieve, pressing down on the solids with the back of a spoon. Discard the solids. Stir in the salt and sugar to taste.

To freeze the granita, follow the method on page 16.

Chile

serves 4 to 6

THIS GRANITA IS REALLY
HOT, YET SWEET, TOO,
SO I WOULD SERVE IT
AS A PALATE CLEANSER
OR FINAL COURSE.
FOR AN EXTRA OOMPH,
DRIZZLE ON TEQUILA OR
VODKA WHEN SERVING.

1 medium to hot fresh red chile,
such as (from milder to hotter)
ancho rojo, serrano, or habanero

3 cups water

1/2 cup plus 1 tablespoon sugar

Zest and juice of 3 limes

Cut the chile in half. Use a sharp knife to remove the seeds and pith and chop the flesh very fine. Wash your hands well; the "hot" molecule in chiles, capsaicin, can make your skin and eyes burn.

Stir the water, sugar, zest, and chile together in a saucepan and simmer for 3 minutes.

Remove from the heat and add the lime juice. Cool to allow the chile to infuse the mixture.

To freeze the granita, follow the method on page 16.

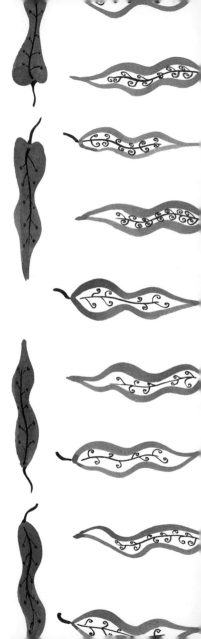

Cucumber
& Mint

serves 4 to 6

2 large (14-inch) English cucumbers

Juice of 1 lemon

3 tablespoons sugar

$1/3$ teaspoon salt

$1^{1}/_{2}$ tablespoons finely chopped mint leaves

1 cup yogurt or dry white wine (optional)

Peel the cucumbers and chop them into a food processor. Add the lemon juice, sugar, and salt; puree until smooth.

Strain the mixture through a fine sieve, stirring with a spoon but not pressing all the solids through; discard the solids.

Mix in the mint and yogurt or wine, if using.

To freeze the granita, follow the method on page 16.

THIS REFRESHING GRANITA MAKES AN IDEAL APPETIZER TO SERVE BEFORE A MEAL OR BETWEEN COURSES. I LIKE TO MIX IN YOGURT OR WHITE WINE BEFORE FREEZING.

Sparkling
Beet

serves 4 to 6

LIKE BORSCHT, THIS
GARNET-COLORED
GRANITA IS DELICIOUS
TOPPED WITH SOUR
CREAM. MIX IN A DROP
OF VODKA IF YOU LIKE.

2 cups homemade or store-bought fresh beet juice

1 to 2 tablespoons sugar

2 tablespoons fresh lemon juice

1 cup sour cream

If you make your own beet juice, keep the skins on when you run them through the juicer, since that is where most of the nutrients are stored. Store-bought beet juice is just as good.

Stir the sugar into the beet juice until it dissolves. Mix in the lemon juice.

The sour cream can be mixed in now or dolloped over after serving.

To freeze the granita, follow the method on page 16.

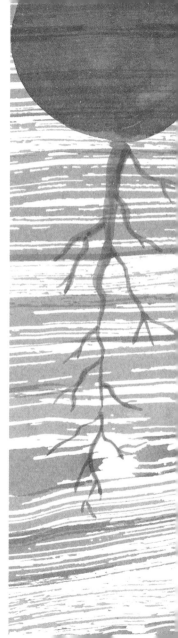

Nuts, Coffee & Chocolate

Chocolate

serves 4 to 6

THIS IS A CREAMY
GRANITA FROM
THE ITALIAN TOWN
OF CATANIA. IT'S
ESPECIALLY DELICIOUS
WITH WHIPPED CREAM.

FOR THE CLASSIC
VIENNESE COMBINATION
CALLED MOCHA, MAKE
HALF THE QUANTITY OF
CHOCOLATE AND STIR IN
2 CUPS OF ESPRESSO
COFFEE BEFORE
FREEZING. MOCHA IS
THE NAME OF THE
PORT IN YEMEN FROM
WHICH COFFEE WAS
FIRST EXPORTED.

4 cups water

$2/3$ cup sugar

1 cup ($2^{1}/_{2}$ ounces) natural unsweetened
best-quality cocoa powder

Put all the ingredients in a medium saucepan.
Turn on the lowest heat and, when the mixture
starts to bubble at the edges, thicken it over
the heat, stirring, for just 1 minute longer.
Allow to cool.

To freeze the granita, follow the method on page 16.

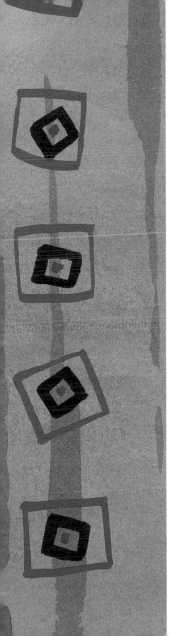

Chocolate
& Rosemary

serves 4 to 6

2 sprigs fresh rosemary

4 cups water

²/3 cup sugar

1 cup (2½ ounces) natural unsweetened
best-quality cocoa powder

Bruise the rosemary with the back of a spoon
to help release its fragrance.

Follow the procedure for Chocolate on
the opposite page, adding the rosemary to the
saucepan with the other ingredients.

Let the rosemary infuse until the mixture has
cooled and chilled, and then remove it just
before freezing.

To freeze the granita, follow the method on page 16.

FRESH ROSEMARY AND CHOCOLATE MAY SEEM LIKE A STRANGE MARRIAGE, BUT THE COMBINATION IS SURPRISINGLY DELICIOUS AND EVEN ADDICTIVE.

ANOTHER EXCELLENT PAIRING IS CHOCOLATE AND ORANGE. TO MAKE IT, GRATE THE ZEST OF 1 ORANGE INTO THE CHOCOLATE MIXTURE AS IT'S HEATING. I LIKE TO SERVE THIS WITH SMALL STICKS OF CHOCOLATE-COVERED CRYSTALLIZED ORANGE PEEL.

Pistachio
& Rose

serves 4 to 6

THIS DELICACY IS
ONE OF MY FAVORITES.
THE HINT OF ROSE
WATER GIVES IT
A TURKISH FLAVOR.

SET ASIDE A LARGE
HANDFUL OF NUTS TO
CHOP COARSELY AND
MIX INTO OR SPRINKLE
OVER THE GRANITA
WHEN YOU SERVE IT.

2 cups raw, shelled, unsalted pistachio nuts (see sidebar)

6 cardamom pods, crushed, hulls discarded

4 cups water

1 tablespoon rose water

9 to 10 tablespoons superfine sugar

Process the pistachio nuts with the cardamom until finely ground. Add 1 cup water and whiz to a fine paste. Add the remaining water and whiz until you have a beautiful green milk.

Over a bowl, line a large sieve with very fine cheesecloth. Pour in the pistachio milk and let it drip into the bowl for several hours or overnight in the fridge, stirring from time to time.

When the liquid has drained, pick up the edges of the cheesecloth to form a bag. Squeeze gently to wring out the last drops of liquid. Stir in the rose water and sugar until the sugar dissolves.

To freeze the granita, follow the method on page 16.

NUTS, COFFEE & CHOCOLATE

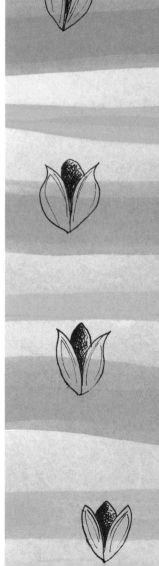

Coffee

serves 4 to 6

THIS CLASSIC GRANITA
IS SO MUCH MORE
REFRESHING THAN ICED
COFFEE! ITALIANS SERVE
COFFEE GRANITA WITH
A SPOONFUL OF WHIPPED
CREAM AND SOMETIMES
SCOOP IT INTO A
BRIOCHE. I LIKE TO MAKE
BATCHES TO KEEP IN THE
FREEZER THROUGHOUT
THE SUMMER TO HAVE AT
BREAKFAST, AFTER
LUNCH, OR AFTER DINNER
WITH WHIPPED CREAM
FLAVORED WITH
SAMBUCA, AN ITALIAN
LICORICE-FLAVORED
LIQUEUR.

2^1/$_2$ cups water

^{1}/$_2$ cup finely ground espresso coffee

1 teaspoon lemon zest

5 to 6 tablespoons sugar

1 tablespoon lemon juice

If you have an espresso machine, make 2^1/$_2$ cups of extra-strong espresso. Otherwise put the water in a saucepan, add the coffee grounds, and bring to the boil. Immediately turn off the heat.

Add the lemon zest and allow to infuse for 5 minutes. Strain through a coffee filter.

Mix in the sugar while the coffee is still warm. Stir in the lemon juice.

To freeze the granita, follow the method on page 16.

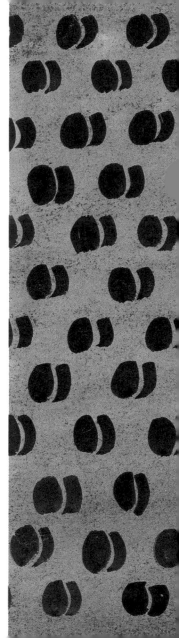

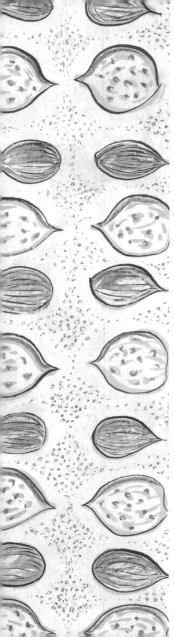

Almond

serves 4 to 6

2 cups whole blanched almonds

4 cups water

1 tablespoon orange blossom essence (optional)

6 to 9 tablespoons superfine sugar

Finely grind the almonds in a food processor. Add 2 cups water and blend until the mixture turns to a paste. Add the remaining water and blend to a milk.

Line a large sieve with very fine cheesecloth and place it over a bowl. Pour in the almond milk and let the liquid drip, covered, for several hours or overnight in the fridge.

When nearly all the liquid has drained, pick up the edges of the cheesecloth to form a bag. Squeeze gently and wring out the last drops of liquid. Add the essence, if using, and stir in the sugar until it dissolves.

To freeze the granita, follow the method on page 16.

THIS RICH AND CREAMY GRANITA IS A CLASSIC FROM THE ISLAND OF SICILY, WHERE IT IS OFTEN EATEN WITH WARM BRIOCHE. IT TAKES SOME SQUEEZING, BUT IT'S WORTH THE EFFORT.

THE GRANITA HAS A VERY DELICATE PERFUME AND FLAVOR. IF YOU WANT AN EVEN MORE ALMONDY FLAVOR, ADD 2 OR 3 DROPS OF ALMOND ESSENCE TO THE MILK.

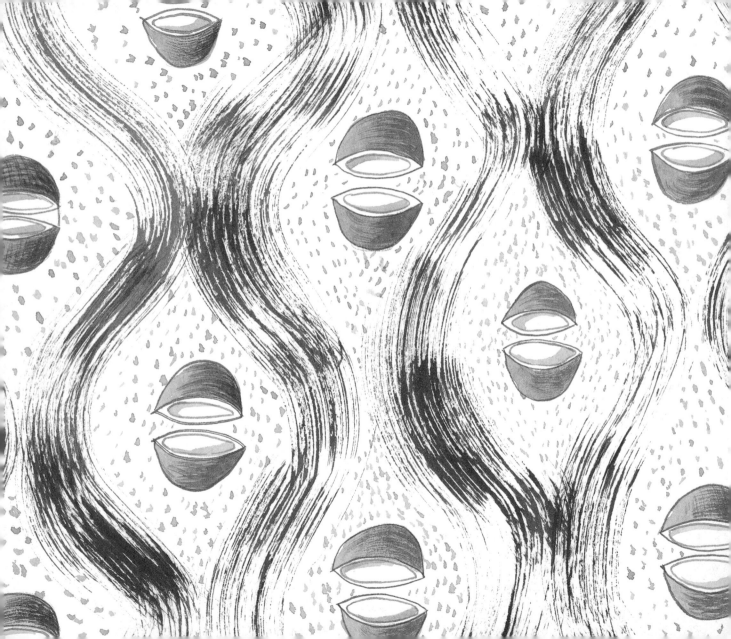

Coconut
& Lime

serves 4 to 6

1¼ cups water

⅔ cup sugar

One 13.5-ounce can unsweetened coconut milk
(2 cups)

Juice and zest of 1 lime

Place the water and sugar in a saucepan and simmer until the sugar dissolves. Remove the pan from the heat, allow to cool, and stir in the coconut milk. Add the lime juice and zest.

To freeze the granita, follow the method on page 16.

THIS SNOW WHITE GRANITA IS DELICIOUS WITH A SPLASH OF RUM.

MAKE SURE THE COCONUT MILK IS A HIGH GRADE, SINCE THE CANS VARY IN QUALITY.

Herbs, Spices & Flowers

Saffron
& Honey

serves 4 to 6

IT IS WONDERFUL
TO WATCH THE COLOR
OF THE SAFFRON
GRADUALLY TURN THIS
GRANITA FROM
CADMIUM YELLOW TO
CADMIUM ORANGE—
LIKE A MOROCCAN
SUNSET.

TRADITIONALLY,
MILK IS NOT USED
IN A GRANITA.
BUT I HAVE BROKEN
THE RULE HERE.

¹⁄₃ teaspoon saffron threads

6 cardamom pods

3 cups whole milk

6 to 8 tablespoons orange blossom honey

2 tablespoons rose water

Crush the saffron with the back of a spoon.
Crush the cardamom pods and discard the
husks. Combine the saffron, cardamom, milk,
and honey in a medium saucepan. Slowly bring
the mixture to a simmer.

Remove immediately from the heat and allow
the mixture to infuse until it is cool. Add the
rose water.

To freeze the granita, follow the method on page 16.

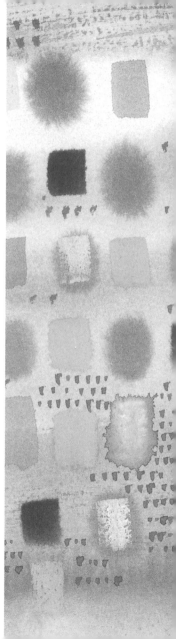

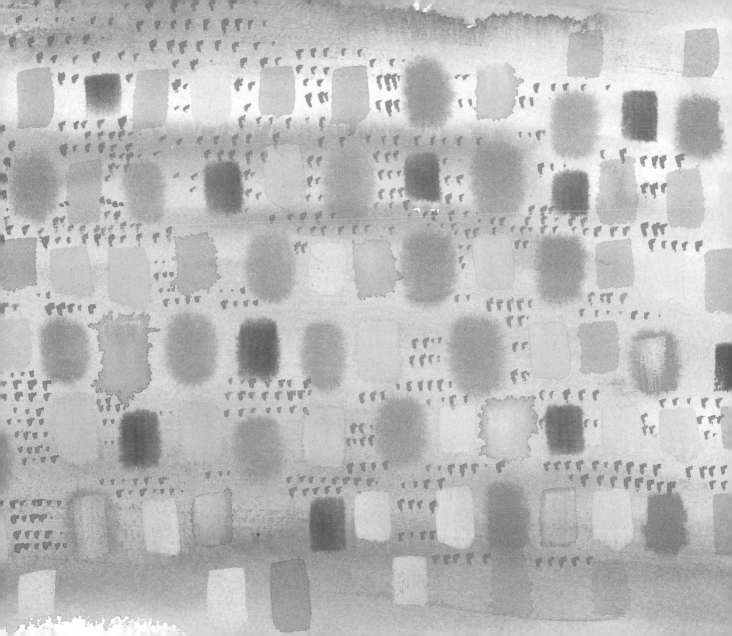

Mint

serves 4 to 6

3 cups water

$^{1}/_{2}$ cup sugar

1$^{1}/_{2}$ cups fresh mint leaves, loosely packed

3 tablespoons lemon juice

In a saucepan, simmer the water with the sugar until the sugar dissolves.

Remove from the heat and submerge the mint leaves in the syrup. Cover and infuse until cool or overnight, if you crave a more intense flavor. Strain and mix in the lemon juice to taste. Taste and add more sugar if needed.

To freeze the granita, follow the method on page 16.

To freeze the granita, follow the method on page 16.

SO REFRESHING AND SIMPLE. TRY VARIOUS MINTS—PEPPERMINT, SPEARMINT, PINEAPPLE MINT, OR PENAG ROYAL.

A FEW EXTRA MINT LEAVES MAKE A LOVELY GARNISH.

Lavender & Honey

serves 4 to 6

THIS GRANITA TAKES
ME TO THE MIDDLE OF
A LAVENDER FIELD
IN PROVENCE, OR INTO
A BUBBLE BATH!
THE ADDITION OF
CHAMPAGNE LENDS
AN EXTRA REFINEMENT
TO THIS VERY
LADYLIKE GRANITA.

GARNISH WITH
A LAVENDER SPRIG
IF YOU LIKE.

2 cups water

1/2 cup lavender honey
(3/4 cup if using Champagne)

1 1/2 tablespoons lavender flower heads

3 to 4 tablespoons lemon juice

1 1/2 cups Champagne
(optional)

Gently simmer the water, honey, and lavender together in a saucepan for just a minute. Cover and set the mixture aside to steep until cool.

Strain out the flowers. Stir in the lemon juice to taste and the Champagne, if using.

To freeze the granita, follow the method on page 16.

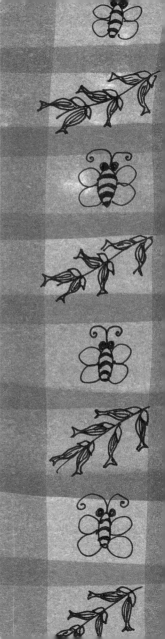

Hibiscus

serves 4 to 6

1 cup dried hibiscus

5 cups water

1 heaping tablespoon finely grated ginger (optional)

¹/₂ to ³/₄ cup superfine sugar

Put the hibiscus in a medium saucepan with the water and ginger, bring to the boil, and simmer for 3 minutes. Let the mixture cool, then chill covered. Strain out the hibiscus and stir in the sugar until it dissolves.

To freeze the granita, follow the method on page 16.

THIS TART AND SWEET SCARLET GRANITA IS INSPIRED BY THE ANCIENT EGYPTIAN DRINK CALLED KARKADE. IT IS BEAUTIFUL ON ITS OWN, BUT YOU CAN ALSO TOP IT WITH FRESH CHOPPED FRUIT SUCH AS MANGO, LITCHI, OR STRAWBERRIES.

LOOK FOR HIBISCUS IN MIDDLE EASTERN OR JAMAICAN STORES, WHERE IT IS SOMETIMES CALLED SORREL, FLOR DE JAMAICA, OR KARKADE.

Rose Petal

serves 4 to 6

ADDING A LITTLE ROSE
WATER ENHANCES
THE VERY DELICATE
FLAVOR OF THIS GRANITA,
AS DOES ROSE PETAL
JAM. FOR A LOVELY
DESSERT, GARNISH WITH
CRYSTALLIZED ROSE
PETALS AND CREAM.
IDEAL FOR A WEDDING!

YOU MAY ALSO WANT
TO TRY EXPERIMENTING
WITH ELDERFLOWER,
JASMINE, ORANGE
BLOSSOM, OR VIOLET
PETALS.

4 cups water

¾ cup sugar

Petals of 3 scented red or pink roses (unsprayed)

1 to 2 tablespoons rose water

2 tablespoons freshly squeezed lemon juice

2 to 3 drops red food coloring (optional)

½ cup rose petal jam (optional)

Place the water and sugar in a medium saucepan and bring to a boil. Remove the saucepan from the heat when the sugar has dissolved. Drop in the rose petals.

Cover and allow the mixture to steep for an hour or two.

Strain out the petals (I like to leave a few in), then stir in the rose water and lemon juice. If you like, add the food coloring and rose petal jam.

To freeze the granita, follow the method on page 16.

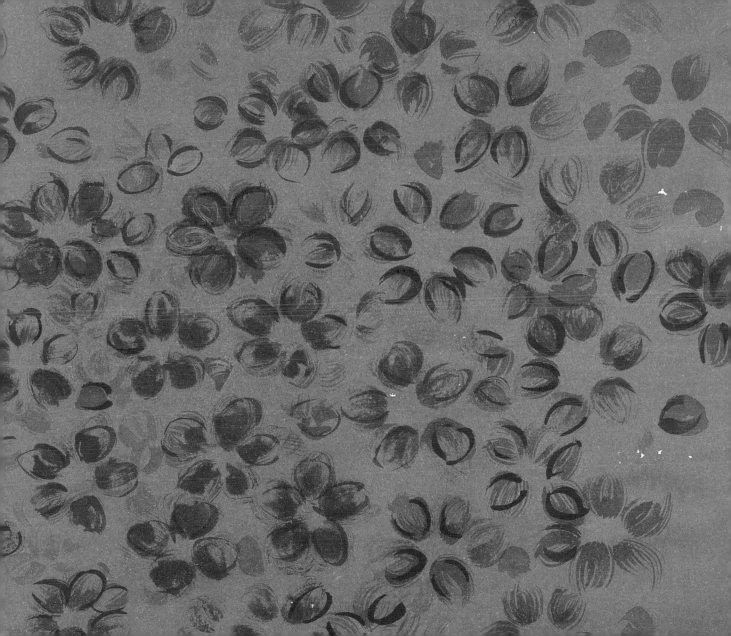

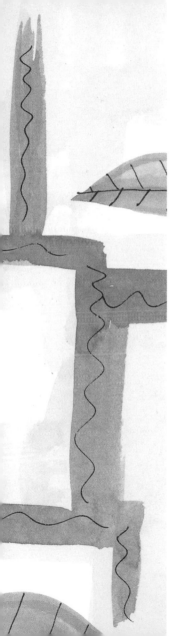

Basil & Orange

serves 4 to 6

½ cup plus 2 tablespoons sugar

2 cups water

Zest and juice of 3 large oranges

½ cup fresh basil leaves, very finely chopped
(2 heaping tablespoons after chopping)

Juice of 2 lemons

Put the sugar, water, and orange zest in a
medium saucepan and heat until the sugar has
dissolved. Stir in the basil and the orange
and lemon juices. Allow the mixture to infuse
for at least 1 hour or overnight.

To freeze the granita, follow the method on page 16.

AN UNUSUAL
COMBINATION, BUT
ADDICTIVELY DELICIOUS.

TRY SUBSTITUTING
FRESH TARRAGON LEAVES
FOR THE BASIL AND
YOUR GRANITA WILL
HAVE A MORE PEPPERY,
ANISELIKE FLAVOR.

Lemongrass

serves 4 to 6

THIS PALE
TRANSLUCENT
GRANITA HAS
A VERY DELICATE
FRAGRANCE.

4 large fresh lemongrass stalks

$^1/_2$ cup sugar

3 cups water

4 tablespoons fresh lemon or lime juice

Cut the tops and trim the bases off the lemongrass stalks; discard the thick outer leaves. Slice the stalks into $^1/_2$-inch pieces and place them in a food processor with the sugar; blend together to a paste.

Place the paste in a medium saucepan with the water. Heat to just below boiling. Set the mixture aside to cool to room temperature.

Strain through a fine sieve, pressing down on the solids with a spoon to extract all the juice. Stir in the lemon or lime juice.

To freeze the granita, follow the method on page 16.

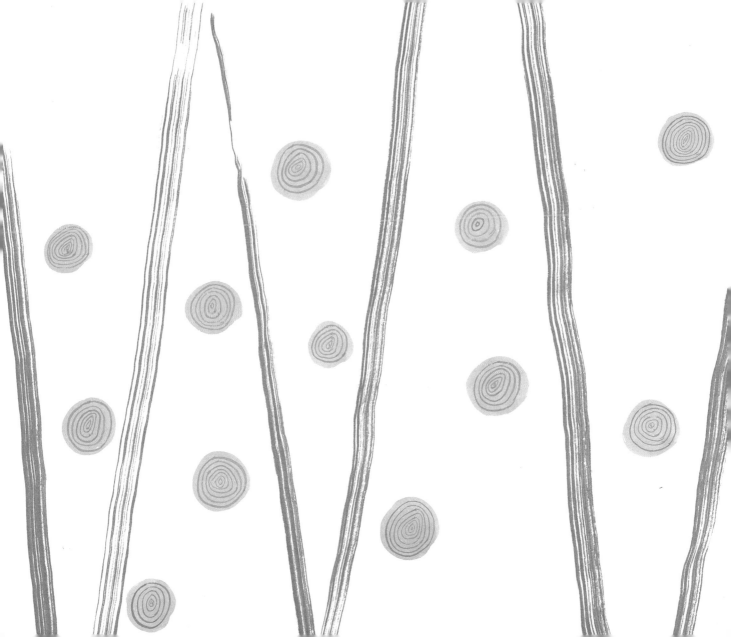

Star Anise
& Grapefruit

serves 4 to 6

²/₃ cup water

¹/₂ cup sugar

1 teaspoon grapefruit zest

4 to 6 whole star anise

Juice of 4 large yellow grapefruits

Put the water, sugar, grapefruit zest, and star anise in a saucepan and simmer for 5 minutes.

Remove from the heat, allowing the star anise to infuse until the mixture is cool.

Remove the star anise (save them to decorate the granitas at the table) or leave them in if you prefer a stronger flavor. Mix in the grapefruit juice.

To freeze the granita, follow the method on page 16.

STAR ANISE IS THE FRUIT OF A TWENTY-FIVE-FOOT CHINESE EVERGREEN MAGNOLIA TREE. BESIDES IN CHINA, THE TREE NOW ALSO GROWS IN INDIA, JAPAN, AND THE PHILIPPINES.

FOR AN EXTRA SPIKE, YOU CAN PASS AROUND PERNOD OR ANOTHER ANISE-FLAVORED LIQUEUR FOR PEOPLE TO DRIZZLE OVER THEIR GRANITAS.

Tamarind

serves 4 to 6

4 cups water

3 ounces tamarind pulp with seeds ($^1/_2$ cup)

6 tablespoons sugar

In a medium saucepan, boil $2^1/_2$ cups water with the tamarind pulp for about 10 minutes, or until the pulp has fallen apart.

Strain the mixture through a fine sieve and discard the solids.

While the tamarind mixture is still warm, stir in the sugar and the remaining $1^1/_2$ cups water. Taste. If the flavor is too strong, add more water or sugar to taste.

To freeze the granita, follow the method on page 16.

Ginger

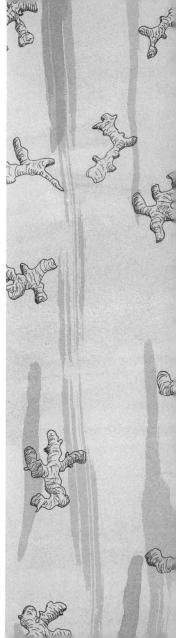

serves 4 to 6

SO HIGHLY CHARGED—
SO VERY DELICIOUS.
BUT IF YOU PREFER A
MILDER TASTE, SIMPLY
REDUCE THE AMOUNT
OF GINGER.

1 heaping cup peeled and coarsely chopped
fresh ginger (about 6 ounces)

1 cup sugar

3 cups water

Zest and juice of 3 lemons

Combine the chopped ginger and the sugar in a food processor and whiz to a paste.

Place the ginger paste in a medium saucepan and add the water and lemon zest. Heat the mixture to a simmer, then remove the saucepan from the heat. Cool to room temperature and put it in the fridge to chill. The longer the ginger sits in the pan, the more intense its flavor will be.

Strain the mixture through a fine sieve and discard the solids. Mix in the lemon juice.

To freeze the granita, follow the method on page 16.

Indian Chai

serves 4 to 6

1¹/₂ inches fresh ginger, chopped

8 cloves

1 large stick cinnamon

6 cardamom pods, crushed

1 bay leaf (optional)

¹/₄ teaspoon freshly grated nutmeg (optional)

3 cups water

¹/₂ cup sugar

2 tea bags

²/₃ cup whole milk

Combine all the spices, water, and sugar in a saucepan and simmer for 5 minutes.

Remove the pan from the heat and add the tea bags. Steep for 3 minutes, then remove the tea bags. Set the mixture aside until cool, or overnight for a stronger flavor.

Strain the mixture through a fine sieve and discard the solids. Stir in the milk.

To freeze the granita, follow the method on page 16.

THIS EXOTIC GRANITA HAS A COMPLEX LAYERING OF SPICES. IT IS INSPIRED BY THE TRADITIONAL MASALA CHAI. ENJOY IT ANY TIME OF DAY.

Herb Garden

serves 4 to 6

Use any one of these or
other fresh herbs:

Four 6-inch sprigs rosemary

Six 4-inch sprigs tarragon

Four 6-inch sprigs mint

Four 6-inch sprigs thyme

20 large basil leaves

20 large sage leaves

10 large lime leaves

6 large dried or fresh
bay leaves

½ to ¾ cup sugar to taste

3 cups water

1 cup dry white wine

3 to 4 tablespoons
lemon juice

Rinse the herb and bruise it with the back of a
spoon. Place it in a saucepan with the sugar and
water. Simmer until the sugar dissolves.

Remove from the heat and add the wine. Cover
and leave to cool. Infuse overnight in the fridge.

Add the lemon juice and strain, leaving in a few
sprigs or leaves (they will look like leaves frozen
in the snow). Garnish with extra fresh leaves.

To freeze the granita, follow the method on page 16.

THESE HERB GRANITAS
ARE REALLY SPECIAL!
ONE SPOONFUL AND YOU
TASTE EVERY HERB AT
ITS PUREST AND FULLEST.
I SOMETIMES MAKE
THREE DIFFERENT HERB
GRANITAS AT ONCE
(IN HALF QUANTITIES)
SO EVERYONE CAN ENJOY
A LITTLE OF EACH.

Tea Leaves

serves 4 to 6

EXPERIMENT WITH
COMBINATIONS OF YOUR
FAVORITE TEAS—
AND TRY SOME NEW
ONES, TOO. EARL GREY
AND JASMINE GIVE
GRANITAS A DELIGHTFUL
FRAGRANCE, WHILE
GREEN TEA AND SPEARMINT
IS A MOROCCAN
FLAVOR BLEND.

$3\frac{1}{2}$ cups water

2 tablespoons loose tea or 6 tea bags

$\frac{1}{2}$ to $\frac{2}{3}$ cup sugar
(it will taste less sweet when frozen)

2 to 3 tablespoons fresh lemon juice

Bring the water to the boil and pour over the tea
leaves. Let the tea infuse for at least 5 minutes,
to taste (but not much longer than 8 minutes
or the tannins will turn it bitter).

Strain the infusion. While the tea is still warm,
stir in the sugar until it dissolves, then add
lemon juice to taste.

To freeze the granita, follow the method on page 16.

Wines & Spirits

Peach Bellini

serves 4 to 6

½ cup water

½ cup sugar

Zest of ½ lemon

4 large ripe white peaches, such as Babcock,
White Lady, Blushing Star, or Silver Logan

Juice of 1 lemon

1½ cups Prosecco or other sparkling white wine
or Champagne

Heat the water, sugar, and lemon zest in a
medium saucepan. When the sugar dissolves,
remove the pan from the heat.

Peel the peaches by immersing them in boiling
water for about 1 minute and then slipping off
their skins. Cut the peach flesh into chunks.
In a food processor, puree the peaches, sugar
syrup, and lemon juice. Chill the puree, then
stir in the Prosecco. Freeze right away.

To freeze the granita, follow the method on page 16.

To freeze the granita, follow the method on page 16.

INSPIRED BY THE
COCKTAIL MADE FAMOUS
AT HARRY'S BAR IN
VENICE, THIS GRANITA
IS AT ITS MOST SUBTLE,
DELICATE BEST WHEN
IT'S MADE WITH RIPE
WHITE-FLESHED PEACHES.

Tequila
& Lime

serves 4 to 6

2½ cups water

¾ cup sugar or more to taste

Zest of 2 limes

Juice of 4 limes

6 tablespoons tequila

THIS POPULAR DUO FROM SOUTH OF THE BORDER HOLLERS OLÉ! SERVE IT STRAIGHT FROM THE FREEZER.

Combine the water, sugar, and lime zest in a saucepan and bring to a boil. Remove the pan from the heat when the sugar has dissolved.

Allow the syrup to cool down before mixing in the lime juice and tequila.

To freeze the granita, follow the method on page 16.

Burgundy Wine

serves 4 to 6

2/3 cup water

1/2 cup sugar

Zest of 1 orange

Juice of 1 large orange

2 cups Burgundy wine

Place the water, sugar, and zest in a saucepan. Bring to a boil and simmer until the sugar dissolves.

Remove from the heat and allow the mixture to cool. Stir in the orange juice and wine.

To freeze the granita, follow the method on page 16.

THIS GRANITA, WHICH SHOULD BE SERVED STRAIGHT FROM THE FREEZER, IS IDEAL FOR A HOT EVENING ON THE LAWN OR A SHADY PORCH. TRY TOPPING IT WITH FRESH MIXED BERRIES.

Spiced Wine

serves 4 to 6

1 cup water

1/2 cup sugar

6 cloves

2 cinnamon sticks

1/4 teaspoon ground nutmeg

Zest and juice of 1 orange

Zest and juice of 1/2 lemon

2 cups red wine, such as Zinfandel, Shiraz, or Pinot Noir

Pour the water into a saucepan and stir in the sugar, cloves, cinnamon, nutmeg, orange zest, and lemon zest. If desired, add any other spices you want to try. Simmer for 3 minutes, then stir in the orange and lemon juices and the wine. Simmer again. Remove the pan from the heat and allow the mixture to cool and chill.

Strain the liquid into a shallow pan and discard the solids.

To freeze the granita, follow the method on page 16.

HERE'S A REFRESHING FINISH TO A RICH HOLIDAY MEAL. REALLY, IT'S GOOD ANYTIME.

HAVE FUN AND EXPERIMENT WITH OTHER SPICES, SUCH AS STAR ANISE, ALLSPICE, AND BLACK PEPPERCORNS.

YOU CAN MAKE THIS INTO A SANGRIA-STYLE GRANITA BY MIXING IN CHOPPED MACERATED FRUIT AFTER FREEZING. BUT REMEMBER TO SERVE THIS STRAIGHT FROM THE FREEZER.

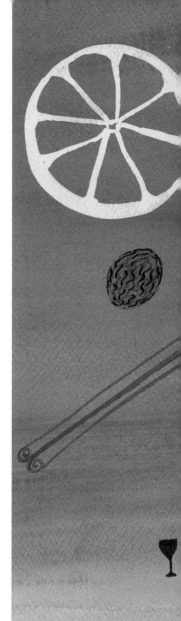

Sauternes

serves 4 to 6

1 cup water

¼ cup sugar

Zest of 1 orange

2 cups Sauternes

In a saucepan, heat the water with the sugar and orange zest until the sugar dissolves. Remove from the heat.

When the mixture has cooled, stir in the Sauternes.

To freeze the granita, follow the method on page 16.

THIS GRANITA MAKES A GRAND DESSERT. SERVING FRESHLY DICED OR SLICED APRICOTS, PEACHES, OR MANGOES, ON TOP OR ON THE SIDE, WILL GIVE EXTRA COLOR, TEXTURE, AND FLAVOR.

LIKE THE OTHER GRANITAS IN THIS CHAPTER, SERVE THIS ONE STRAIGHT FROM THE FREEZER.

SAUTERNES CAN BE FROZEN ON ITS OWN WITH THE ZEST AND WITHOUT THE WATER, BUT IT FREEZES ONLY TO A SLUSH.

Champagne

serves 4 to 6

WONDERFUL BETWEEN
COURSES OR AS A LIGHT
DESSERT TOPPED
WITH RASPBERRIES OR
SLICED STRAWBERRIES.
FOR A NICE VARIATION,
MIX IN 1 CUP OF
PUREED FRESH PEACHES,
PINEAPPLE, OR PASSION
FRUIT BEFORE FREEZING.

MAKE THIS GRANITA
WHEN YOU HAVE AN
ALREADY OPEN BOTTLE
OF CHAMPAGNE.
ENJOY THE CHAMPAGNE
AGAIN RATHER THAN
DISCARDING IT.

2 cups water

¾ cup sugar

Zest of 1 lemon

Juice of 1 lemon

3 cups Champagne, chilled

Bring the water, sugar, and lemon zest to a boil in a medium saucepan. Boil for 3 minutes, then remove the saucepan from the heat. Allow to cool before adding the lemon juice.

To freeze the granita, follow the method on page 16.

When the mixture is almost frozen, scrape it with a fork and stir in the Champagne. Re-cover the pan and allow it to freeze again.

Serve the granita straight from the freezer.

ACKNOWLEDGMENTS

My warmest thanks are for Terry De Pietro, who was my guiding spirit for this book. He tasted every granita and discussed every design.

I also want to thank my mother, Claudia, for instilling a love of food and the good things in life. She also never tired of our daily transatlantic phone conversations, discussing the merits of a particular fruit, herb, or spice.

I am very grateful to Ann Bramson for her enthusiasm and support and for seeing this project through, to Vivian Ghazarian for her sensitive eye, to Deborah Weiss Geline for her understanding, to Nancy Murray for her production expertise, to Amy Corley for her spirited publicity efforts, and to Peter Workman for his vision.

Special thanks to Judith Jones for steering me in the right direction. She has always been an inspiration.

I am very grateful to my father, Paul, for his boundless appreciation and encouragement, and to my friend Brie Burkeman for her kind and valuable professional advice.

Family, friends, and neighbors, thank you for tasting granitas at a moment's notice!

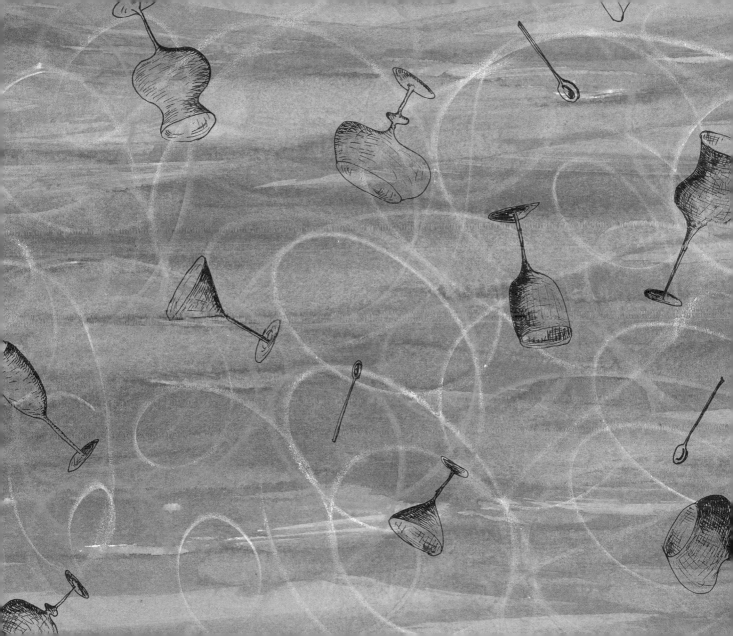

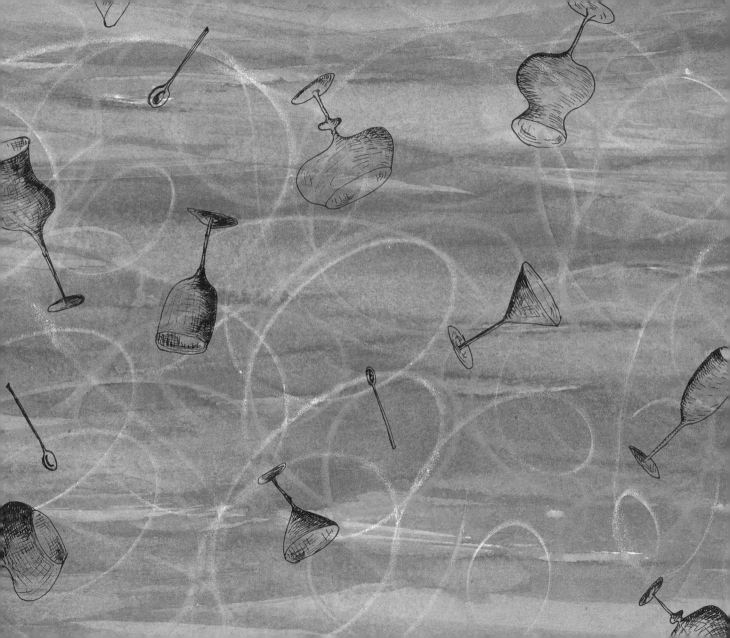